Times in
MY MIND

Times in
MY MIND

JANLISA PARRIS

ARPress
ILLUMINATING IDEAS.
EMPOWERING VOICES

ARPress
45 Dan Road Suite 5
Canton MA 02021

Hotline: 1(800) 220-7660
Fax: 1(855) 752-6001

Ordering Information:
Quantity sales. Special discounts are available on quantity purchases by corporations, associations, and others. For details, contact the publisher at the address above.

Printed in the United States of America.

ISBN-13:	Paperback	979-8-89356-792-2
	eBook	979-8-89356-793-9
	Hardback	979-8-89356-794-6

Library of Congress Control Number: 2024909333

Contents

Dedication

She was the only one who loved me. Promise you that! I loved her so much too! Then, she was my everything and some. When that smile came in the doors, I was loved again. Yet, when she left me, I felt unloved in my environment. There they were sitting in front of the TV, while I sat on the couch behind them by myself. Yet, not caring until she came home again. That is why I dedicate this book to my grandmother (Mrs. Lillie Mae Whitehurst-Shelley: June 28, 1929 – January 10, 2014). Her present was to weep for. Her voice was the sound of rain at night that put you to sleep. Grandma Lil was and still the thought of her calms me and makes me alive again. She was the truth, because she spoke it! My mother, not having the money to buy me a royal blue prom dress, and yet of course my Grandma Lil brought it. Grandma Lil brought most of everything (events, uniforms, etc.) I needed and wanted while I was in high school and as well as school, period. Her heart was so huge, and that's why mine is so big too. I learned everything from her. Whenever I went somewhere and needed to tell someone, she would be the first phone call. When I needed an alarm to wake me up, she would be it. When she promised me something, she came through, by any means necessary. I couldn't do nothing wrong and of course I didn't intentionally, anyway in her eyes. I may have been spoiled by her, but it was a good spoil. Just to be in her presence or talking over the phone was deemed that I was SAFE, and the spirit of her still watching over me is priceless. Grandma Lil touched everybody's life in an awesomely great way. She was so much loved by all she encountered. I used to go to work with her if she had to work on a Saturday and in the summer months. The loving and kind doctors she worked for used to give us big trash bags of clothes, ever since we were young children up through high school. It meant everything to my siblings and me. We were so appreciative. My Grandma Lil retired from being a domestic housekeeper and she was great at it! The doctor and his family are just like our cousins. Not only did my grandmother work for the doctor; she was everything and some to them too. We all share so many moments and memories of such a gorgeous African-American Queen. We all miss her and thanked her while alive, and we forever will love our Grandma Lil.

Special Dedication

My "Friend/Sister Forever", as we would always greet one another!

Tee always said, "Friend, when are you going to write your book", and stayed in my ear!

Tee was supposed to write the 'Foreword', but she didn't have the strength (my God!), but she was excited to know my other "Friends Forever", wrote it. Yet, Tee continued to motivate me through her good and bad days and looked forward to reading my book.

Well, "Friend Forever", it's published, and rest assured my Angel, I have your copy!

Tee brought out the motivation in me when I didn't have the strength; and even over our 39 years of friendship. We were dedicated to our bond and what it meant to even have one friend in this lifetime. I thought I couldn't go on without my friend, but she wouldn't have that!!! I know she is with me, because her spirit is in my walk, my talk, and my heart! I could write a book about our friendship, but you all aren't ready for it! I can hear her hollering-laughing, "Write it Friend, Write it," then we'll start bringing up all our stories!

No, I'll keep it between us, what you think friend (in spirit)!

We confined to each other, hold heartedly. When we felt one another's bothered-spirit, the phone rang, then we'll start our church humming-helm and bust out singing, then she'll say, "ok friend, leave it alone, and we'll start hollering-laughing! Yes, she had the voice of the 'Angel' she was! I always talked about her presence in my life, in counseling sessions. We brought each other through some times by our spiritual connection to God! No matter where we lived, we were really just right there with each other.

Friend, I miss you so darn much that I must stay in the presence of God!

"Friends Forever"

Queen, Mrs. Tamura E. Williams-Hedgemond
(September 14, 1968 - May 6, 2020)

Foreword

Fall 1986 on a cool, calming afternoon as Donnetta Davis, a Birmingham, Alabama, native, now an educator in Atlanta, Georgia, and LaTanya Sellick, a Cleveland, Ohio, native, now a surgical assistant in Nashville, Tennessee, were strolling through the campus of Alabama State University (ASU), headed toward Abercrombie Hall, one of the most popular female dormitories on campus, approaching with anticipation of who would be our new roommate, and we could hardly wait. As we were whispering and giggling coming down the long freshly polished hall, we came upon a cracked door and the first thing we noticed was a freckle-faced with an inviting smile young lady.

"Hello," we stated, and she responded with "Hr."

We looked at each other confused, then she repeated with a "Hi." We then recognized the Missouri accent. It was also the beginning of a thirty-year-plus friendship.

We knew someday Janlisa would have a story to tell because of her uniqueness and a person that was persistent from the first day we met; a book is perfect. From day one she spoke from her heart, which sometimes came off as too aggressive, but as our relationship grew we knew there was a soft teddy bear behind that "big roar" she displayed. There were so many nights we sat around and told stories of our hometowns. When we listened to Janlisa's stories (good or not so pleasant) about her upbringing in St. Louis, Missouri, it continuously reminded us how strong she was. In addition, we would admire the love she exhibited toward her son, "Marlon," the cutest little boy that sometimes strolled the campus as well when he came for a visit. The strength Janlisa showed us after having a child in the 80s (not an easy thing to do) and still wanting to better herself by obtaining a college degree was all we needed to continue focusing on our own positive desires. We can't remember a time when we called on "Jan" for maybe a little change to purchase a late-night snack, a jacket to wear on a cold night, or even a shoulder to cry on when nothing seemed to be going right. Her perseverance and approach to difficult times is the energy and moving force to the longevity of our friendship.

After the initial introduction of our friendship, we knew our relationship would last through thick or thin. Having "Jan" as our selfless protector against any situation, but of course we would have to remind her to sometimes put herself first, which never really worked. Even though we were from different walks of life, each one us had a slice of the pizza that gave the fullness to a thirty-year- plus friendship. Therefore this book, in our opinion, is overdue but still just in time.

Preface

My mother was very hateful toward me. She left me as a baby, upstairs in my crib, wet and shit running up my back, screaming from the top of my lungs, said Grandmomma Lil. But my grandmother rescued me from the turmoil. Then my mother put me off as another man's child, who really loved me as his oldest, and he went to his grave never knowing the truth. But my grandmother was my angel from God. She was always there to comfort me in the midst of all the hard times I had, dealing with my mother's drug habit, yet while caring for her children. If I didn't hear from my grandmother every day, then she was very busy, and that was not many times. There will never be another like her in my life, of course! She always spoiled me, but I guess she knew I deserved it too. She used to call my mother and ask if I could come over to her apartment and help her clean on the weekends, and it was a blessing to get away from the house of hell. Most of my work habits and dedication to learning was due to her teaching and instilling it in me. She meant the world to my siblings and me. Without her in my life, I don't think I would be writing this book, and probably on drugs or an alcoholic. I can't even fathom walking in the streets and selling my soul. I know my grandmother went to her grave worried and stressed over my mother being a drug addict. My siblings and I searched the streets for Momma before we left to see our grandmother out of town. I was one angry and upset human being, because she didn't get a chance to go with us (children, grands, and great-grand) to see our grandmother after her major surgery that took her to her resting place at Flowers Hospital (ICU) in Dothan, Alabama. We all share so many wonderful memories of such a beautiful soul (Lillie Mae Shelley, June 28, 1929 – January 10, 2014). Forever she will be.

Chapter 1

CONSEQUENCES

She wants it all and some. No, it's my mother. All I know is she was raised with her mother and father and both grandparents on each side. They surrounded her with love, because she told me. Oh, and how her father's mother bought her a dress for every day during Easter week. How she had everything, even a little red tricycle, and as she was old enough to ride a two-wheel he bought her a blue one. Yet, back in those days (1946...) her father worked, and things came easy for her as a little girl. She had my grandmother, who was a hard worker too, and from time to time my grandmother picked cotton and gave the money to her mother for her brothers and sisters, while raising my mother. In those days, that was how life was and the norm. Nevertheless, my mom didn't have it bad because all she had to do was go to school, do her homework and chores at her grandmother's house, where they lived. Yet, her father of Hartford, Alabama (Jimmy Lee Shelley, 1922-1979?), went to jail while he lived in New Jersey. He wrote my mother letters, so that he could get pictures of his grandchildren before he got out of jail. My mom moved to St. Louis, Missouri, from Enterprise, Alabama, when my Grandma Lil moved to St. Louis from Newark, New Jersey (Bergen Street), where she worked at Remco Toy Factory. Grandma Lil said that my mother wouldn't even open the letters to read them. My granny opened and read the letters, though. He had gotten out of jail a little before my mother was 32 years old and was killed no longer afterwards. How did my mother become so selfish!

One day, my momma left me in my crib screaming at the top of my lungs with shit running up my back. Thank God for my grandmother, who recused me out of the crib and cleaned me up while she was down the street at my granny's small teenage place and while the adults played cards in the back of the store. That is where it all started for me of the sadness of a child whose mother was worried about herself. She just knew she could count on her mother to take care of me and my brother, while she ran back and forth to Potosi, MO, where I was conceived, and she didn't know who the father was. But lies she told! My grandmother said she was wild and partied all the time.

My grandmother would say she wouldn't even keep the store for her while she took care of business for the store. But all she wanted was my granny to give her money so she could run with her girlfriend to Potosi, Missouri, in the streets and with the man that she claimed was my father (Robert Lee Bell, May 25, 1948 – December 27, 2009). Therefore, I was born with the last name "Bell," then later, before college, she tried to change my name to "Shelley." Come to find later in life my last name change didn't go through back in 1986 and it was still "Bell." But I had two birth certificates and my last name was "Shelley-Bell."

While she was dating (Robert Lee Bell) and putting me off on him as my father, and while having three more children after me, she put the baby daughter off on him as her father too, that was later revealed.

I remember when my brothers and sisters were calling me "white girl," "you albino," "you were adopted," I cried and the name calling had me sad inside a little, and it went on through high school.

Thank God my baby sister, Malenda, met her father and got to know him well. She met her aunt, cousins, and grandparents too. Unfortunately, her father passed away of liver disease from drinking. But, I'm so happy that one of us got to know their biological father.

My mother ought to be ashamed of herself, passing me off on a man who genuinely loved me as his oldest daughter. I gave him the love back as much as I could up until and through his hospice care. I told him, "Daddy, it's okay, you can go, I'm going to take care of Lenny and her kids." He was so worried about his baby girl, whom he did everything for, and it was alright with my soul that he did! Yet so he went, on December 27, 2009, the night I was at a holiday party in which I was trying to take a break from the sorrow. Then I received the call, my father had just passed. I will never forget that night, but I was in time to kiss and feel his warm body before the coroners took him out of Malenda's house.

Chapter 2

LIES DON'T LAST ALWAYS

My sister, Latanya, and brother, Shane, along with one of my daddy's sisters, tried to prove to the bank and judge that I wasn't my father's child. The bank and judge said if my father designated me his banking account beneficiary, it didn't matter if I was blood or not. The moneys went to me after court, because of the fact of the decision made by the judge. Therefore, the bank called me to come pick up the money. I went by my sister Malenda's house to get her to go to the bank and pick up the money, then inside the bank. I turned around to her and gave her all the money. I didn't need the money at all. I didn't even want nothing my husband and I had purchased for his burial.

My father's sister went by the funeral home and told them that I wasn't his daughter and the director of the funeral home contacted me and told me that I had to bring a birth certificate with his name on it, in order for the funeral to be paid for by his sister. I was devastated by all of this. It was so stressful that I had to take a trip out of town to my cousin's house in Montgomery, Alabama. But I went by the funeral home and signed over the rights that I would have nothing to do with the funeral arrangements. This was enough to make a person have a heart attack. Yes, my sister, Latanya, and brother, Shane, were in on it with my aunt. Oh, she's not my aunt, because I'm not my father's child! Yet, I didn't even go to the funeral because I had enough of the mad drama.

I blame my mother for the breakup with my daddy. From what I do know he was a provider. He made sure we ate and lived decent. We lived in a three-story house. Until one day he put me in the first-floor middle room closet to punish me for something my middle sister did. I was always told, "Since you're the oldest you know better." Really, at nine years old. Until that one day he flooded our house while we were in school. He found out my mother was cheating on him. Momma met us as we were getting off the school bus and took us around the corner to his brother's house. They took my father to Malcom Bliss Mental Institution, on the city's Southside (Arsenal Street). He had never been the same man since his release. After that gloomy and confusing day, things were scary. I wish I could say things was happier without my daddy, but it wasn't.

From a house I called home to living with family members to living upstairs in a three-room house from my third to eighth grade years, to living in the whole six-room house, going upstairs from the back outside to the three rooms, where we slept and she slept downstairs with a man I hated, who was controlling of her and us, who was not raising his own children. We didn't respect a nonworking, motorcycle-riding bomb. I couldn't stand him to his core. He didn't even take care of his own children, who lived with his parents, in Black Jack, Missouri.

I remember, before he came to live with us, I'll never forget, he came to his door where he lived on North 23rd Street, in St. Louis, Missouri. I had come on my menstrual cycle while in the eighth- grade gym class and back then, you could walk home, and the school allowed me to. I walked about three miles from Blewett Middle School to North 23rd Street. My mother was at his house while all her children was in school. I knocked on the door and he answered and called my mother to the door. I told her that I had come on my cycle (age 13), while she told me to go home and she would be around to the house. She didn't come until after school was out. She knew I would make sure my siblings were fed, yelling with a bologna sandwich. I did call my granny and ask her to bring me some pads. I told her where Momma was and what she told me when I went to her boyfriend's house.

Well, from what you know about my grandmother, she was on it. She brought me my pads and a douche. She showed and explained to me about a woman on her cycle and after a cycle, of what I should do to cleanse myself. My Grandma Lil was everything and some. Lord, I adored her everything. My Grandma Lil rescued my spirit. I couldn't fathom living without her back then. She came when there was no food, which was often. She brought food, household supplies, which included my pads too.

Chapter 3

RESPONSIBILITIES

One summer, my mom left us with her cousin who lived downstairs from us. She and her (no-good) man went out of town on one of his motorcycle group trips. I still was responsible for us eating and putting on my sister's and brother's clothes to play outside. But while I was playing outside (age 11), a neighbor across the street screamed to "Get Man-Man, he's in the window." The bed was next to the window where he was sleeping, and he had awakened and was looking all the way out the window, where he could look down to the ground. I ran so fast and grabbed him out the window. He was nothing but one year old. He could have fallen out the window and that would have been on me too. God will forever get the Glory! My mother probably would have killed me!!!

Bitch, you think you're better than everybody! Slap… (in my face hard). Tears came down, and not because it hurt. The tears came because I felt she hated me, because she birthed me and when she looked at me I reminded her of a lie! I thank God for dreaming every night. It was an escape of knowing that I was going to get out of this mess. Four more years and off to college I would go. People didn't know the pain, because I always had a poker face and/or most of the time a smile. Lord knows I hated her for what she always did to me. Yes, I was afraid of her. Because I couldn't make a mistake around her. But I stood strong. I felt I wasn't supposed to feel pain. Stay strong, this will be over soon. But, oh, it didn't seem like it. I prayed to God every night just to give me my mind, Lord! But I didn't think I was better than my brothers and sisters. I watched over my siblings and cooked and made sure they were bathed and did their chores so I wouldn't get whipped or slapped in the face. I was tired, you all, but I kept pushing through those four more years before college. Oh, I knew I was going to college.

I couldn't understand the whoopings because we were good kids and had manners. But not good at letting the (no-good) man try us as his children, because he wasn't raising his own.

She let him discipline us. While him and her was downstairs in the three-room part of the house and their bedroom was in the middle room. They smoked weed and no telling what else. She left us upstairs in the cold, before the gas was turned back on. We put enough covers over us, and we would be alright with one heater in the middle upstairs room for all five of us. We got up in the morning and got ourselves ready, and she didn't even come upstairs to see if we were dressed properly. You-know-who had to make sure everyone was dressed and decent to go to school. Yes, me! But I was proud to give them that love and support. They are my siblings, my hearts, and my friends. I wanted the best for them, and at the same time I wanted to run away. Then, what would happen to them?

But I fought him off my siblings when that (no-good) man would whoop them. That mean fucker always tried to make us out to be some bad and undisciplined children. Yes, he tried to whoop me too, but I would fight, scratch, and pick up things to hit him with. I would cuss him out and fight until my mother came to hit me too, to show herself approved by him.

She didn't see the pain in my heart. All she saw was trying to please (no-good) him and that she was doing her part by letting me talk back to this evil fucker. God knew I hated him too much, that I could kill him. Oh, yes, I came at him with a knife to kill him, when he would whoop me over again. We got a whooping for not saying good morning, good evening to him. Who the hell did he think he was? He would want us to call him Daddy. Hell, to the knaw, knaw, knaw, over my dead body and my siblings'.

His own three children disrespected him when he wasn't even raising them. They were good, disciplined, and well-mannered children until they got around (no-good) him, they called Daddy still. It seemed like the two sons was angry with him always. He munched off my mother's welfare check. That was all that was coming into the household as far as I knew. If it wasn't for our Grandma Lil, Grandpa Bill, and Grandparents Bell, we wouldn't have had new school clothes, shoes, underwear, socks, and even money for pads. Even my father/daddy (Robert Lee Bell, 1948-2009) would sneak and give us money, and when we called him on the phone to come see us he would have to come, and we would meet him at the corner. He only lived around the corner with his parents. My mother was afraid he would hurt her and (no-good) him. I was trying to get us out of Hell, by calling Daddy all the time, so he could catch them both and kill them. Yet my daddy had been labeled schizophrenic (mental disorder) after leaving the institution.

Just to bring all this back is horrific!

Lord knows I was glad I was graduating middle school and on to high school. Yet, not knowing we were going to move again to the Westside of St. Louis, right up the street from Soldan High School, where I went and was active in pom-pom, cheerleader, and concert choir. Yes, my mother brought this (no-good) man with us. She even birthed a child by him (boy-child #6). How bad could it get from my sixth- to eighth-grade years? Then came the unexplained whooping and I was still fighting and defending my siblings too, due to if (no- good) didn't get what he wanted out of us. We refused to respect and be his slave children. It did seem as if I was the one getting all the whoopings. I never gave into him. He wasn't going to break me.

The Slaps in My Face

We had some great values instilled in us when our father (daddy) was living with us. We had a lot of aunts and uncles in St. Louis on our daddy's side and they were role models and my mom was a caring mother then. I called my daddy again and again when (no- good) would whoop me or my siblings. My daddy would come from the Northside to the Westside and we would be playing outside when we weren't on a punishment and see him walking down the street. He was trying to get to the (no-good) man my mother called a boyfriend. But just as we would embrace my daddy and tell him some of the things that was going on in the house, my momma would call us back in the gate so that Daddy could go away. But, just seeing him for a moment was everything.

Our other option was calling our Grandma Lil and Grandpa Bill (step-papa) and all a grandad could be. But when we did call them, they would come right up Delmar Blvd. from Deperes Ave. My grandma would bust through the door and go off on my mother and that (no-good) man. After my Grandma Lil and Grandpa Bill left, my mom would slap me and tell me not to ever tell nothing that went on in her house. Well, I didn't care what she said, I always called my Grandma Lil about everything that happened in the home.

I remember one day my cousin from Wentzville, Missouri, came to visit with his wife. That night when we all were asleep, my cousin came in the living room when I was sleeping on the couch and pulled and lifted my PJs to look at my privates. I had awakened and pretended I was asleep and that I didn't feel anything. But I hated that bastard ever since, and yet not telling anyone about that night. If I had told my mother about what had happened, she would have said I was lying and probably slapped me.

All through high school there was whoopings, fighting back with knives and fighting (no-good) him off me and my siblings. I didn't care nothing for him. I told him I hated him. My mother would feed him first, then feed us, by calling us to the table after she fixed his meal. This (no-good) man didn't even work to pay any bills. We always had our gas, electric, or phone off throughout the years while he was living with us.

Even though I had an older brother, he would be so angry. One day he had gathered his friends and they was going to kill that (no- good) man. They were waiting on him to go to the back of the yard and get on his motorcycle. I begged my brother not to do it. He (no- good) and my mother don't even know that. I didn't want to lose my big brother to a (no-good) man.

It didn't matter that I was the tutor for my siblings at the kitchen table after school. My mother and the (no-good) man didn't acknowledge my intellect.

Chapter 4

WATCH WHO YOU BLAME

I became pregnant at age 15 years old and had my child (son) at 16 years old. I was a junior upon conception going to the twelfth grade. I was still cheerleading up to seven months. My friends would ask me if I was pregnant and I said, "No." So, I kept on cheering. One day at school my cheerleading and the basketball coach brought me into an empty room and asked me if I was pregnant. So, I said yes, at five to six months then. Yet my mother was being asked by her friend up the street from us if I was pregnant. Not knowing that she had money for me to have an abortion. But I could just see my mom telling her, "No, she's not pregnant."

But one morning when Soldan High School's concert choir was going to go to state and sing, my momma came in the bathroom as I was putting my dress over my head and I froze and she said, "You pregnant." I said, "Yes, ma'am." She immediately told me to put on some other clothes so she could take me to the doctor's office. She took me to her OBGYN. My momma just had another child by this (no-good) man on February 1, 1985. How could I tell my mother I was pregnant when she was pregnant too? How could I tell a mother that I was trying so hard to get away from? How could I let my sisters and brothers down? How could I let a (no-good) man see me pregnant? How could I let my grandparents down? How could I let my aunt and uncle down, who lived in Alabama? Mostly, how could I let myself down?

One Friday school evening, I had gone over my Grandma Lil's house to get a breather and to just be around her. My mother and the (no-good) man came to get me, without me knowing it. I was crying because I didn't want to go back to that house. So, when I got in the vehicle he reached back and slapped me. God know if I had a gun or knife, he would have been a dead duck. My mom didn't say anything. There I was, seven months pregnant and in rage.

The weekend of our family gathering in early July 1985, with all my cousins from out of town (Alabama, Detroit, and New Jersey) in the huge backyard of my great aunt and uncle's in Wentzville, Missouri, my great uncle got wind of that (no-good) man slapping me and he went off on him and was going to hurt him and he went off on my mother too.

My son was born on July 29, 1985, to me and the man who had pretty much date raped me. I was on my menstrual that evening when I was supposed to be at Junior Achievement with my two girlfriends. But instead I went to his house and my girlfriends and I were supposed to meet up when they had come back from the program that was in the old Sears building on Kings Highway and Page Blvd. I told him that I was on my menstrual, but he didn't care. He turned the light off and started taking off my bottom clothes and he date raped me.

I told a few people early on and then social worker/therapist/ psychiatrist and besties. I had no ideal then it was date rape, I didn't know what date rape was back then. Yet, some would say I should not have been fast. But all young girls some way or another was fast back in high school that I knew about.

God knows I tried to put the pregnancy off on another man that I had met later afterward, because he was so good to me. I even had him see the baby and his mother said that wasn't her child's son. I knew that! I told the truth and told the biological father that he needed to come see his son all within the same week. I am so thankful to God that I made the right decision. He did come to see his son and that was all, and the last time seeing him was when he graduated from high school.

Nevertheless, I graduated from Soldan High School and my aunt and uncle from Alabama came to get me and my son. My son was raised by my aunt and uncle, and they did a great and awesome job in my son's upbringing. I am forever grateful and indebted to them. My son had a plethora of family and friends helping in the upbringing that my aunt and uncle saw to them being in his life. They loved me too. My aunt and uncle wanted to adopt my son and they did.

I attended Alabama State University, Harris-Stowe State University, St. Louis Community College, and Webster University, all where I received up to my second M.A. degree and several certifications and certificates. School was my out! It allowed me to be free! January 8, 1992, I had gone into the United States Army and remained part of it until July 22, 2005.

Chapter 5

GIVING UP ON THE PAIN

Eight years after having my oldest son, I had my baby boy, whom my oldest named. During my pregnancy with my youngest son, his father had slap-punched me in my face. I had just got off from my United States Military office job (Killeen, TX). I had come into the apartment that evening and when I told him that you tell a dog to shut up, before I knew it he was out of the shower and up on me, while I was standing out on the balcony that opened from the dining room and kitchen. I still had my uniform on with my boots. So, when this bastard hit me and I lifted my head up and he must have seen in my eyes that he would die that night he ran, grabbing his pants and out the front door.

Let me tell you, I walked back in the dining room and took the back of my left hand, lifting the table off the floor, and threw it against the wall. I reached for the butcher knife out of the knife block and went straight out the kitchen and threw the knife as he was turning the corner to the front door. The knife stuck in the wall and then fell to the floor. If there was not a curve to the front door, that knife would have penetrated his ass. I ran and picked up the knife and ran out the door to catch him, but he had gotten in the car already and sped off.

All of this because his coworker dropped him off up the road when a tornado was coming near the fields where he was walking home. His coworker was trying to get home too. I usually picked him up, but I had to stay behind at the office due to a meeting the colonel had with other officers. I still went to the trailer construction area where he worked to see if he was still there waiting on me.

I truly loved this man dearly. I was pregnant with his child and I was going to tell him that evening, before he slap-punched me.

Then one day, he said to me, "I just hit you one time." Once was enough, bastard!!!

I had just lost my stepsister (Alethia Marie Harris, April 1964 – Dec. 1990) of Black Jack, Missouri; well, that's what we called each other, because our two youngest brothers were our siblings. Yet, she treated me like her sister. She was shot dead by her fiancé on their front lawn. I knew not only before then but ever, I wasn't going to let a man hit me without repercussions.

Texas didn't play about a man hitting a woman. Therefore, my son's father went to jail by turning himself in. He was let go and had to pay for anger management classes. It didn't matter that I was having his child; I left him because he was going to hit me again and might wind up killing me. I had already mentioned how I would kill him if I did get back with him and he hit me again. But I had a child that didn't ask to be here, and I was responsible for his wellbeing and to keep myself sane and a part of his life. I wasn't going to let love keep me bound to him. The way I fell in love was the way I was going to fall out of love. Protecting me was protecting my child.

Chapter 6

SAVING YOURSELF
IS NOT ENOUGH

Yes, school kept me because I had to finish what I started. I have been a tutor, mentor, adjunct, high school, and substitute teacher. I was on a mission and didn't know I was going to be an educational- holic. I made life work, all while raising my siblings too. Through it all I was running them to school to enroll them in middle school to high school. Taking off work and going to take them to the doctors' offices. Picking them up from school. Helping with homework.

My mother was always gone on her crack mission. She was nowhere to be found until the holidays, she would show up. I was a nervous wreck worrying about her in the streets. It was crazy out there. We would be watching the news, just to not hear the police didn't find our mother dead. But I thank God for my Grandma Lil for letting us live with her and back and forth when I had to move in between having my own place. She was there to rescue us all for all we ever needed.

Between my two sisters, Malenda Shelley and Latanya Shelley-Sacus, and Grandma Lil, they were trying to do their best, helping to take care of my three baby brothers when I asked for assistance. But the sole responsibility was on me. Even my sisters needed my mentoring (motherly) love and support. Without thinking about it, I took care of them all the best I could while taking care of my child (baby son).

I didn't know what tired was. God gave me the energy every morning to get up and go through another day. Not knowing how it was going to turn out. But I was up for the challenge. I worried about my siblings and mother out in the streets. I didn't want to bury a mother, but she was doing a disbelief of a mother with seven children. We did see her after a week or three weeks at a time.

Because she was my siblings' mother, I had to get her to go to the welfare social security office to get their Medicaid renewed and for social security cards, birth certificates, etc., to have in my possession. I had to buy my brothers' clothes and my grandmother did too, all while living with us, when Momma didn't have a place of her own.

Yet I was the head of them three boys because I was the elder sister with the job and car. From running around to the clinic and dentist appointments, I was getting their haircuts and making sure they ate. I know my siblings were missing their mother, as well as I was too.

Christmas came around through the years and it was sad, yet a mix of emotions because we knew she (our mother) was going to leave and wander out in the street again for her habits and addictions. I could not lose my brother and sister as years went by and they became grown men and mature women. I was still the one they called on and looked for me to make it happen when they asked for something needed or wanted. I worried how I was going to make it happen, but I made it happen and between my grandmother and I we made it happen.

I could never save. I made ends meet to care for my son and put him through private school and running him to all his school plays, sport activities, and me going to classes and getting so much needed relief by going to the bootcamp classes and other classes at the YMCA. All while going to reserve training once a month and two weeks' active duty training out of the years.

Going to church was a way maker. I don't know how I was going to keep on keeping on without building the strength up in my spirit and soul. My son loved Sunday School, Wednesday evening bible study, and church. It didn't matter if I was raising my child, I was responsible for my siblings because they looked up to me. Lord knows I wasn't trying to replace their mother and my mother too.

I tried hard to not let my siblings interfere with me raising my son separately. I tried to keep his life separate from my raising and caring for my siblings. I made sure I lived in a secure apartment where it was safe. He had his own bedroom wherever we lived. He had quality clothes and shoes. I kept him active in sports in his years and great mentors and leaders in his life. Before and after high school, when he was automatically active in a sport (football), he had friends just like him that were into sports. I was trying so hard to keep him in healthy environments.

A friend of mine, and she's a friend still today, she gave me food out of her parents' deep freezer to take to my siblings in Wentzville, Missouri, where they lived with my mother. I came home from college one summer at my grandmother's house. Oh, how I will never forget that, and I told my friend I would forever be indebted to her kindness and loving deed. She was a blessing and even to his day.

Chapter 7

LEAVING IT ALL BEHIND

Before I left to go to college and leave my siblings, it was very painful knowing I had to leave them. I wanted a better life for my son. The focus of my aunt and uncle coming to get me and my son was for me to go to Alabama State University. My aunt and uncle didn't give up on me and I wasn't giving up on me because I had a child. My aunt and uncle attended ASU too. My uncle graduated with a degree in Mathematics. I had a handful of cousins at ASU when I attended. I couldn't wait to go to college to learn and grow and, most of all, get away from the horrible conditions I was living in. My mother had move from the Westside back to the Northside on Alice Street and that was the worst thing she could have done.

My mother had brought the (no-good) man with us, then she got rid of him and met this other man and he was on drugs too. We woke up on the floor where we slept. We didn't have beds to sleep on. The heat was off, and we all were upstairs in one room under a lot of covers, where we made pallets. I knew I was leaving with my baby boy to Alabama, so I worked almost every day at The Fudgery in the newly opened Union Station in Downtown St. Louis. I bought all my clothes for college. Yet, my mother would take my money that I brought home. I would buy my clothes and leave them over my grandmother's house.

Then I would go home with what I had left over from my checks. Lord knows I didn't just give my mother my money.

This other man that was living with us was just as horrible as the other (no-good) man. He went under my sister Latanya's nightgown while she was sleeping, and she awakened to catch him. He had the nerve to tell his war story to my little sister, Malenda. My mother had her nerve too, to tell my sister not to sit on his lap after she brought this fool in the house.

My sisters would have to call our stepsister to bring them food to eat, while Momma was gone and knew they didn't have anything to eat in the house. It was six children left in the house after I left to go to college. There was also my sister Latanya's husband (Keith Sacus, Mar. 16, 1965 – Dec. 23, 2018) who my mother signed papers to marry him at age 17. Social Services had gotten involved because there was no gas on during this winter. My family had to use a propane stove to heat up the downstairs, where they slept on the floor.

I blame myself for anything that happened to my siblings while I was away in college.

I sent my siblings money from college. It came from my refund checks and work study checks and/or the many jobs I worked after classes (The Limited, Shoneys, Cracker Barrel, Assembly Line, etc.). It was just a piece of something coming from me that made me feel a little at ease knowing that they could buy some new clothes and shoes for school.

Chapter 8

IF I DIDN'T KNOW BETTER

I had met this young man that was so sweet and kind to me. He sent me money, jewelry from Germany, where he was stationed in the United States Army. When he got leave to come home, back to Enterprise, Alabama, he would come to see me, and we would go to the football games at Alabama State University and classics with my cousin and friends. This man was a dream come true, that I thought. But I was in college and he would have to go away again. I will always respect and love him for being the best he could to me when he could. I didn't know exactly what I had. How could I? I didn't have a constant father figure role model. But I wish nothing but goodness and peace over his life, because he tried to love me unconditionally. I thank God for that experience with him, because I know how I want to be treated. Oh, his parents were just as kind and loving too, and I see where he received and learned from.

I remember, while I was in college at ASU, my father (Daddy) would write me. He had awesome penmanship and sense enough to write his daughter. It meant so much to me. Least someone was thinking about me and missing me. Yes, he sent me money too. This man was the only father (daddy) I knew. I figured Daddy had gotten his mind back because he wrote me. Yes, he called at times in the dorms. "Janlisa!"

22

they called out. "Your father is on the phone." Oh my God, it would be the best moment of the day. Unlike someone shouting, "Janlisa, your mother is on the phone." No, she called one time and it was bad news while I was in college (ASU); I mean once. I received calls from my grandmas, granddads, siblings. It was enough comfort from their calls to carry on my week or weekend after them calls. Even when I called my siblings, to hear their voices too.

I remember, when I was in college, my baby sister, Malenda, telling me that my mother climbed in her own house window to steal her coat and unborn baby clothes that my sister had bought new. My mother and her was tussling at the coat, trying not to let her take the coat. They were living in Wentzville, Missouri, at the time in The Heights community, and my great aunt lived down the street. She helped my siblings a lot by feeding them most of the time. My siblings had a host of great aunts, uncles, and cousins who lived in the same small town helping them, which was my Grandma Lil's sisters/brother/brother-in-law/sister-in-law/niece/nephews. Wentzville is 45 minutes from St. Louis, Missouri, which is up the road to me.

My siblings had to endure our very own mother stealing their clothes and coat.

My siblings told me that they couldn't even go to school without a fight because somebody would say something bad about our crackhead momma. Our mother was a disgrace to her children and other family there in Wentzville, Missouri.

When you mentioned one of my great uncles' or aunts' names to a police officer, then that carried weight when something went wrong with my siblings in school or anywhere in Wentzville. Oh, how embarrassing my mother was to the entire family. But she didn't care if she was/could get high.

Just hearing all this drama over the phone and when I came home to visit from ASU was so heartbreaking. I tried to concentrate while away from my siblings, but it was very hard to. I was waging war over all the karma in my mind. I prayed to God to give me my mind all the time since a young age of 11 years old.

I wanted to demonstrate to my siblings that school is very important. I wanted them to finish high school, middle school, grade school so they could go to college too. I was praying and studying, at least trying to study. All I can say is I passed my classes at ASU; it wasn't what it should have been, though. I managed to keep my financial aid, though. Lord knows I read my bible before I went to bed and listened to music to stay on track in school.

I remember, I was called by my mother. I had moved off campus in the beginning of junior year (December 1989) to live with a God-fearing, kind, and sweet young graduate and a senior who were dedicated members of Delta Sigma Theta, Incorporated. But, nevertheless, while I was lying down in my room, my roommate brought me the phone and it was my mother, saying that my stepsister, Alethia Marie Harris (April 1963 – Dec. 1989) was killed by her fiancé. Lord knows I had just talked to her that week and told her what we were going to do when I came home to visit for the Christmas holidays. I couldn't believe my stepsister was dead. I got off the phone with tears pouring down my face. Yet, I went to sleep and woke up wishing I had dreamed what I knew from the night. It was true and real! I decided that I wasn't going home, because I didn't want to remember her in a casket. I wanted to remember the last time I saw her and the last time we talked.

Because I wouldn't come back to school if I had left to attend her funeral, I decided that next day all in less than 24 hours that I would not go home to the funeral. Instead, I went that weekend to my boyfriend's family's home to Mobile, Alabama, with him. Today I have no regrets for my decision either and never had any.

Later that summer of 1990, my boyfriend and I had broken up because he decided to sow his royal oats (venturing out to other women). Yes, he hurt me so bad. I couldn't believe it, for a long time, because we were one of the campus' (ASU) known couples. I did think it was something he had to do, being that I was his first (lover). He let me keep the car (black two-door Monte Carlo) to go to work, which he had worked hard last summer to buy because he got tired of me catching the bus to and from work after my classes. He was a man of love, kindness, respect, laughter, and just a fun guy. He treated me like the queen I am.

I just knew he would be my forever man, husband, guy, but not. His parents and siblings were so kind and caring and they loved me unconditionally. I thank them all for sowing in my life of love, support, and kindness that was generosity, which pierced my heart forever.

Then as the summer of 1990 was coming to an end, I met this young Army Air Traffic Controller from Fort Rucker, Alabama, who soon became my husband on November 15, 1990, to an annulment on January 21, 1991. I had to get his First Sergeant to come with us to the courts, because he didn't want to get an annulment. Don't judge me!!! The only thing we had in common was being brother/sister of Masonic and Order of Eastern Star. Yet, I can't say he didn't love me. He was very controlling, and I could not handle it!

The second semester of 1991 was when I was taking six classes (ASU) in the Computer Science and Mathematics program. I wanted to be initiated in Delta Sigma Theta, Incorporated, that spring semester, but those classes had me bound and not being put on probation with financial aid. I should have gone through with the process of becoming a Delta, because I failed that semester classes. Too much had gone on and I couldn't concentrate that semester. My siblings were going through changes with my mother and her drug addictions by moving back to Wentzville.

Chapter 9

EXPECT THE SUN TO SHINE

Therefore, I decided to return home (I was a confused soul) to St. Louis, Missouri. I stayed with my Grandma Lil once I returned home. But before I left ASU, I knew it was going to be easy leaving. I had taken the ASVAB test for the Military. I went home ready to join the United States Army.

But before I went into the Army, I went to St. Louis Community College to take a Calculus course to add to my continued degree seeking at ASU. I went into the United States Army in January 1992. I continued my education after Active Duty Army and during my years in the Army Reserves.

No matter how full my plate was and runneth over, my mother still was nowhere to be found. When my mother lived in Wentzville in the Hidden Valley community, I said my three little brothers were tired of them not being able to go in the refrigerator and find no food for nutrients. Yes, because my mother would go shopping and then take the meats out the freezer to sell them for drugs. She did this the whole time she lived in Hidden Valley.

I remember, my sister telling me that they lived with friends who were like sisters to my mother. My baby sister, Malenda, had alopecia at the time, and I was told that the kids would pull her scarf off but lo and behold, my middle sister, Latanya, would beat they asses. Also, my sister's best friend too would whoop they ass. I really don't know why they would even want to touch my baby sister, because Latanya didn't play about her family being bullied. There was a sense of protection over my siblings too. Latanya didn't allow no one to even bad mouth her siblings or they would get that butt whooped. Everybody knew Latanya, because she was the fighter in the neighborhood and schools she attended. She loved to fight and even would fight my battles in grade/middle/high school. My mother was a fighter too and worse than Latanya. They both were alike when it came to defending family. I just wish my mother would have taken some of her viciousness to defensiveness and loved her siblings enough to protect and care for us.

Shot in the Head

When my middle baby brother was shot in the head and lived to tell about it. In 2002, my mother was nowhere to be around or reached by phone. But boom, she appeared at the hospital after the word got across north St. Louis to find my mother, "Jean." My little brother was going through. His father (no-good) didn't care about him in trouble because of the way he treated him when he asked to come live with him in his grandma's 15-room inherited house in Black Jack, Missouri. He said no, he couldn't come live with him. My brother suffers from alcoholism.

Chapter 10

NOT LOOKING FOR WHY

My baby brother was sleeping on a thick blanket on the living room floor. My Grandma Lil always slept on the couch and it still runs in the family. Nevertheless, in the middle of the night, in a two-room- one-bath apartment on Enright Ave., in St. Louis, Missouri, my baby brother would crawl in the next room where my son and I was sleeping and slide his hand under the cover. I would jump up and say, "What the fuck are you doing, get your ass back in the living room and go to sleep." Then my Grandma Lil said, "That's what he was doing in here." I got up the next morning and talked to him about that wrong behavior.

Well, he must have learned this wrong behavior because someone had done it to him the same way, while living with my mother when she had a place. By him being the youngest child of seven siblings, he was the last one to live with my mother. Therefore, everywhere she went, he was right there with her up through middle school, until we took over his wellbeing. He did go to middle school around the corner from my Grandma Lil's apartments.

Shaking My Damn Head

No telling if my mother owed for a piece of crack while they were sleeping through the night. This is what my sisters, Malenda and Latanya, always said and we believe it to this day. See my brothers, all four, love them some Annie Jean Shelley (Momma), and if someone had touched my little brothers while they were asleep and they were awakened by someone touching them.

My God!

It bothers me today that if it happened to my young brothers, then why wasn't she paying for what she let happen knowingly to her own sons? I was so happy that other family stayed in the same neighborhoods.

I remember, I went to Wentzville, Missouri, one Christmas Day, and really my brothers didn't have gifts under the tree, because whatever my mom did buy she sold for her crack habit. My great aunt, who lived down the street in the Hidden Valley community, had cooked Christmas dinner, like always. We went to her house for dinner.

I remember, my brother was in the hospital for alcohol poison. I couldn't tell him not to long for his mother and father. They both were near, just not there for him. My heart pained for his troubles in his head. My youngest brother just was there, yet being taken care of. Yet we did our best to keep him loved, but there is no comparison to a sister and a mother.

Lemon-Cheese

When my mother finally came to my grandmother's house in off the street for a Christmas holiday, my mom baked a seven-layer lemon cheesecake. It was delicious too, being that her recipe came from my great aunt. It was great seeing my mom after weeks of being in the streets and not even a phone call from her. My grandmother was very happy to see her too. Her baby boy was happy to see her as well. He was on the basketball team during the school year. Even though I was working and in college, and raising my baby son, it didn't matter to my mother. She was all about getting back in the streets to get her high on three days later and not returning until after the New Year. I am sure she celebrated with a great high with her crack associates.

My mother knew about everybody on the Northside of St. Louis, per say. It is the old neighborhood where we grew up until I was off to high school. It was the place where my mom and siblings moved back to after she finally left Wentzville, Missouri. How could she, though, but I should know not to ask that, because it's where her crack was plentiful.

I remember, how she cussed her mother out so bad that my Grandma Lil would just cry and then give her some choice words and of what God loved. I would have to tell my momma that she must leave this apartment now. My momma was a horrible woman when she didn't get what she wanted, and she still is today.

Chapter II

BREATHE IN – BREATHE OUT

Today, yes, today, 2020, at age 73 years old, my mother/momma is still on crack rock. After so many years on that crack rock, you would think she would have stopped by now. That is some strong stuff that has a hold on my momma. She goes out now for a day, or two or three, and gets her high on. Then she returns around the family for about two weeks and goes out for a couple of days in the middle of each month, but in the beginning she's gone for at least five days.

I have had several intense conversations with the raised voice. Because I have let the wondering about why she still does what she does, while all her children are fully grown. The baby, 35 years old now, is still on the back of my head just lingering. No, I'm not stressed anymore about her crack addition.

I just, I guess, how can a grown great-grandmother still be on crack? How can she look at her seven children, grandchildren, and great-grandchildren and not be a non-crack-addict woman? Is she proud of us all strong and still made it out of her environment from being raised in it? Can it be that she cares or doesn't care? That is what I'm damn confused about.

Annie Jean Whitehurst Shelley has a giving heart from what I know about her character. I thought maybe after her son was shot in the head she would stop. Maybe after her mother passed away. Maybe after her grandbaby's passing (Malenda's daughter). Maybe when her baby boy went to juvenile for touching his niece. Maybe when she was moving all over the city and county. Maybe when she got raped and let go. Maybe when her sons and daughter, Latanya, was on crack and heroin. How can she sit down and talk to him about living a crack/heroin life is not the way to go? She can't!!!

I can sit and listen to her now about the addiction, but way earlier in my years of trying to understand why she kept the addiction going I wouldn't have.

Yet and still pretty much there is nothing to say to me about her reasons why she kept the addiction up. She has been selfish. We didn't ask to be here.

I am judging my mother. Do I have a reason to judge? She put a very dark place in my spirit and yet I still love her and respect her as my momma and mother.

I don't know if I'm angry still with her for being on crack or just being the person she was before she got on crack.

I am just hollow inside about her still being on crack at age 73. Yet I'm not worried and all disgusted about her these days.

Does my momma feel hollow inside too? What is she fighting inside? God had really blessed my mother for 56 years, from the time I knew she was on crack.

I remember, thinking that when my grandmother had her small store, and someone put something in my mother's drink. My granny said my momma was stronger than all the men that was trying to hold her down. She was like a raging bull, my granny said. But the hospital pumped the poison out of her.

I was thinking, could that have been it, that started her addiction of other things while she had a baby girl? Has she been feeling empty since? Was it a thirst she had? Was she chasing after the high from the poison/mickey that was dropped in her drink?

I remember, (1997-98) my friend, told me, "If I had gone through what you've gone through, I would have killed myself." Then I said, "That's why I went through it, because I can handle it." This moment stayed on my mind for all these years. We were coming from Harris-Stowe State College of me seeing a counselor about my class schedule.

I remember, coming home one summer after the second semester ended at ASU, my mother was angry because I wouldn't give her my money. I had worked as a waitress at the (Chuck Berry's Restaurant) in Wentzville, Missouri. She lived with her aunt and uncle in Wentzville. My Grandma Lil and I had come to visit that weekend from St. Louis, Missouri. My mother burst out and said, "That's why Pete (Robert Lee Bell, May 1948 – Dec. 2009) is not your father." I turn around and said I knew somebody was my biological father, at least my spirit told me.

Yet I wasn't going to say anything of how I felt. My brothers and sisters would tease me and say, "You're adopted." Then my mom said to the nurses, "She's not my baby." My mom said I had one string of red hair and bald all around it. Nevertheless, out of anger for her drugs that she couldn't get my money, she humiliated my soul. I tell you, I was hurting bad. Then my Grandma Lil grabbed me and healed me while I cried. Then my grandmother sat me down on the couch and told me that it was true. "Your mother ran back and forth to Potosi, Missouri, every weekend with her girlfriend to see some boy. So, Pete is not your father." My grandmother said it was bound to come out, but this was the wrong way to bring it out! She did tell my mother that she was wrong.

All I can say is that was one of the most horrific days of my life! So, who do I belong to? I felt so all alone. My grandmother told me she ran with some lady, last name "Carter." Damn! Can I stop going through shit? This is some of the feelings that arose in my soul! Asking God for my mind!

Too much is too much, exactly what it means. But not for me. I was handling the things in my life but not without a price of mental disability! Yet, another thing to put in the box so I could keep on moving on through life. So, I stayed at my great aunt and uncle's house, because I wanted to be around my siblings. We slept in the basement, which was clean and very well kept, like the upstairs house. We all slept in one big bed. My great uncle and aunt were the keys to kindness and love unconditionally.

The Ladies

One day in my late 20s, an older woman walked up to me in a department store and just said, "You look rich." I just paused mentally, then I said thank you and smiled back at her. Right then and there, I realized that was God saying, "I'm watching over you; you are not alone, my child, and keep your head up and smile." I felt love come from that woman. No matter what my granny always said, always keep yourself apart no matter how you are feeling and keep your head up. That is how I carried myself, too!!!

I remember, one early afternoon, an old woman saw me strolling my baby son on the walkway of an outside shopping center. She spoke to me and then said, "Who takes care of him?" I paused for a minute and minded my manner that I was getting ready to respond to my elder. So, I started thinking (breathe). But I said with a soft tone, "I do, ma'am." She then said, "He is healthy and happy." I said, "Thank you." I could think was that was a confirmation I'm doing a great job, so keep up the great work.

Chapter 12

PRAYING ALL THE TIME

Lord God knows I can't even tell it all or remember it all. So many nights and days as we didn't know where our mother was. Yes, we prayed, because that's all we knew. I just wanted my siblings to see their mother. I was older and I know the feeling of not seeing or knowing where she was, and it was numb. But for my siblings to be so much younger than me, it hurt badly. Believe me, I know! Yet, we had to hold on to our valuable possessions. I got tired of doing that shit, but I had no choice.

Again, I had a son that depended on me. I couldn't let his uniforms, clothes, shoes be stolen. Yes, I worked very hard to earn a living, like anyone else, but I managed to care for my son and younger siblings too. Malenda and Latanya had children, but they managed to be there when I asked for help with our younger siblings. Grandma Lil was there too, to manage her money and help in with their basic needs and necessities. I didn't know what it was like to be tired. All I knew was going to bed tired and waking up with renewed energy and praying for my siblings to have a blessed day and please no phone calls to come to their schools. But o, I didn't catch a break. I was called to the school for fighting and skipping classes. Yet it happens, yet some boys are going to be boys.

My oldest young brother had dropped out of school, but he managed to get into a place where he received his GED and a trade where he worked for one of the largest airplane part-making companies in St. Louis, MO. I was so proud of him, but I knew he would make it happen. All I wanted was one sibling at a time to get off my back. Later through the years he landed in a bad spot and heroin has been consuming his life since.

I decided to move to Alabama after the federal government was closing some of the federal buildings across the country. I worked at the VA on Goodfellow in St. Louis, but I had to make a move or stay there in St. Louis. I decided to move, and I landed in Montgomery, Alabama, where I moved into a brand-new apartment complex. I had my midnight blue Honda Accord, which my son and I drove to Montgomery with all I had left of what my mother and sister Latanya didn't sell to the antique shop. I had my furniture in the basement of my mother's house. I had to move my stuff somewhere, because my lease was up a couple of months before I drove to Alabama. Yes, my mom and Latanya took lamps, throw rugs, and other items of most my furniture in the county of Bel-Ridge off Natural Bridge Blvd. next to the police station. Then they had the nerve to tell me that I could go buy my own items back. I said, "That's alright, I be damned if I buy my own shit back." I was fired up and hurting so bad. They were bold as hell, knowing I wasn't going to recognize my shit gone from the basement, because that was where my son and I slept, up until it was time to leave out of town.

I will never forget, me and Latanya fought in the kitchen over my items they sold. Yes, I got the best of her, but it hurt my soul to be fighting my sister. That was the first and last fight I ever had too. Nevertheless, she ran outside and starched my Honda Accord up on the driver's side back. I hated her but I love her still, because we are sisters, and I know crack had her too. Again, I knew I was leaving real soon.

Finally, it was time for me to go. Therefore, basically I packed our clothes and my son's toys and other pertinent items that could get in the

Accord and drove to Montgomery, Alabama, where I didn't stay long. It was about nine months at the most, I stayed in Montgomery, before coming back to St. Louis. Yet, I did manage to get on food stamps and interview for a job, because I was collecting unemployment. It was just not enough jobs to choose from for me.

I did manage to be a part of my friend's wedding before I left Montgomery. Yes, I had friends and family nearby too. Unemployment was running out and I knew I was St. Louis bound to stay with my grandmother, where I knew I would always be welcomed.

I knew I would be there for a minute until I transitioned to my own place. It was 1996 when I started working for the St. Louis Board of Education at Sumner High School. As the years passed by, I continued college and worked hard at it. I even managed to get a job as a cashier at a grocery store in the evenings and trained at the Reserves Unit on the weekend, once a month when Reserves time did come around. I was worn out at the end of the weekend, but God gave me the strength and renewed energy each morning.

I managed to move on the Southside of St. Louis City in a duplex off Grand and Magnolia. One Sunday morning, my son and I were headed to church and my car was gone. It was an old four-door Cutlass Cierra that ran well and it was a steal from an older couple's only car that I purchased from the Honda dealership. I just didn't want to purchase a new car, after I had given my car back to the bank after filing bankruptcy. But, if I had known better, I would have kept my car before I filed.

I still had to press on. Therefore, I had to take six buses every day to drop my son off at preschool at the church on Page Blvd. between Taylor and Kings Highway. I took two buses to get there. Then I took one bus to get to work at Sumner High School. Then I reversed and caught the same buses back to get my son and back home. I had received a preschool scholarship from the church as a single parent. God is good! I didn't want my son in the public school system during those days. It would have been too much for a single parent such as a person in my status, I felt. It was too much going on then in the public school system that was not right. I worked at one and I knew the trials firsthand and from the news. I was going to keep my son on the perfect attendance list, because I had to go to work. I was committed to his education and my job.

Again, I thank God for Grandma Lil. She watched him as I continued my schooling at night. I manage to keep Dantrell in private schools and I continued to graduate with three degrees.

These days in the mid-2000s were horrifying when it came to my crack addict mother and her whereabouts.

The Moves

My siblings had moved too many times in four years when I left to go to college at Alabama State University. I left my siblings on Alice Street (north city). They moved to Wentzville, Missouri, at my uncle and aunt's home, then to Grove Street with friends, to 23rd Street (north city), then back to Wentzville in Spur Lane Apartments, to The Heights, then to St. Charles, Missouri, and back to Wentzville in the Hidden Valley senior apartments. My baby sister, Malenda, came to live with me across the street from the St. Louis Airport on Executive South Drive. But they had moved seven different times and just imagine the school changing they had to go through.

June 2007, I met my husband, Darrel Leon Parris, and we were married September 20, 2008. Yet, I had been admiring him at the YMCA for a long time during basketball games. I never thought we would be together in such a way. Yes, I connected with him in the YMCA steam room and the rest is history.

Chapter 13

THE FIRE KEEPS BURNING

I had to go and find my mother, out in the streets for her to try on her dress. I bought her dress at a church rummage sale. It was in a clear plastic hanging bag with other beautiful dresses. When I found her, she was smelly and not looking good. I took her to my sister's house, where she could clean up. We then went to get her some shoes, etc., for my big day. I set up an appointment to get her hair doe for the wedding, but she did her own hair.

No, she hadn't stopped her crack habit at 64 years old, and is still out there in the streets, like a wild child. I know what, that I was determined to have my mother in my wedding. Sad that I had to find her two weeks before the wedding for her to gain weight and get her beautiful skin and complexion back. She gains weight fast once she starts eating well.

My Grandma Lil had moved back to Alabama in 2006, after 40 years of living in St. Louis, MO, since 1967. Of course, my Grandma Lil was coming to St. Louis to be in my wedding, because I wasn't going to have it any other way.

Soon after the wedding was over, my momma wandered around my sister Malenda's house to live and soon afterwards, she was back in the streets feeding her drug habit. My mother had always been homeless, because none of us wanted her living with us for a period due to her stealing.

Everywhere my mother went, she would mess up her public housing or Section 8 vouchers by missing recertification appointments for renewals or having too much traffic in and out her living areas. Just like she had a senior citizen apartment in 2015 through 2017, off Peck and Kossuth Ave. in north St. Louis, but she managed to lose it too. Full of other crack habit people. She tried to say my brother Shane (third from the youngest) made her leave because he was in trouble and he lived with her.

But every time I went to visit her, the folks in her three-room apartment were laying all around, looking straight cracked out. The apartment was small, but at least she had a roof over her head. Where she lived was her old crack stomping ground. Yes, I was scared to visit, so I called her phone or blew my horn, so she could come to the door to meet me, while I got out the car. A lot of times my husband went with me, after we got out of church.

He is her heart too, just like her siblings. Just imagine walking in my mother's apartment and my brother in the bathroom the whole time I was there. I was sick to my stomach that my mom would do drugs with him. She told me that she had never did heroin or crack with him. She said, "That was one of the things I will never do." She is stuck on stupid, because she had the nerve to tell me he was grown and she couldn't tell him what to do.

But ashamed of him, he had gotten out of rehabilitation and was getting his life together for himself first. Then for his three sons and daughter. They got to see him sober again for about three to six months. So darn sad! He had started going to his baby boy's games and living with his son's sister, because they had lost their mother about two years ago.

I would listen to gospel songs to get my spirit back together again. I needed this spiritual growth continuously in my life. Not a day goes by I'm not listening to some gospel or sermon of some sort.

After all the rehabilitation programs my momma had went to for the last 56 years, there is nothing else that can stop her from her crack habits. But she hadn't been a part of one since about 2000. She mentions to me that she's not ever going to get off it, and that she will die from it and it's her life. After I told her that she had never been a role model to her children. She has grandchildren, ten great-grandchildren, and seven children (four generations). I said to her that her grands and greats loved her unconditionally and "why can't you be the title you are and be a role model for them?" But no matter what and how I put it, she refuses to get clean and live a happier life. Because a person can't be happy and been on crack for 56 years.

Her siblings thank God for bringing her home the many days and nights he did. There were plenty times she called us from the hospital, because her bronchitis and asthma were acting up badly through the years.

I really love my mother, but she makes me sick to my stomach all the same time. She is a mess and I remember wishing she would never be seen again. Only so we wouldn't stress anymore. But as the years have passed, she is just so annoying now. Some days I can tolerate looking at her or being around her, but other days I don't want to see or talk to her. Her voice would irk me so bad that she would automatically stress me out. I would have to put on my gospel music or sermons to get myself back together. I would want to go to the gym and most of the time I did just that, to get in the steam, sauna, pool, and whirlpool.

These days, she would mumble under her breath and say mean things like "Fuck you, bitch, and go to hell." Especially after she's been out in the streets and comes home now. She then wants somebody to buy her some cigarettes because she didn't have any after coming off the streets. Well, see, I don't smoke and never have. Yes, I get pissed off when she asks me to buy her cigarettes. Most of the time I would have lied and said, "I don't have any money." The other times I would buy them but want my money back, because I don't smoke or get high. Yes, she made sure when she got money that she would call and say, "Come get your money, I owe you for cigarettes." I would jump up and get in the car to go get my money too. I didn't mess around about my money to my mother.

Chapter 14

PSYCHO DOES WHAT PSYCHO DOES

I remember, my brother Shane was getting himself together but living in the park or at the church front door in the Bellefontaine Neighbors community. It was where his youngest son's mother was living. My husband and I would go in the neighborhood and take him the food his mother cooked on Saturday, for Sunday dinners. We would carry cigarettes to him and some personal items too. We purchased him some seeing glasses, because his broke up. He was considered legally blind without glasses. Believe me, that was the only way he got glasses from us. The church where he was sleeping at on the outside front helped him get a house for his family and put all new furniture (beds, living room, washer/dryer, etc.) in it. I just knew he was destined to make a change for himself and four children. Yell right! That house turned into just a place to do his heroin with his girlfriend, who did it too. Sad, sad, and Sad!

Maybe I shouldn't be disappointed, but I was. Shane was like my favorite, even though he was one of my baby brothers (third from the last). I would not give him anything else after that. I was done! He couldn't ask me for nothing, nada, none of the sort!!! He would call me and have the nerve to ask me for money and buy him some clothes for an interview. His baby boy's mother went to live with her mother. I would tell him to grow up and get yourself together, Shane Travan Shelley. "You have a baby boy that needs you in his life." I would leave him with a message before getting off the phone: "I love you and I'm praying for you." Goodbye!!! I didn't care how bad he begged me for clothes and money because he was going to an interview. He had to fight this battle by himself.

I been down that road before with him. Even he had broken or lost his glasses again and I never bought him another pair online. I told him since he was legally blind that he could go to social services and apply for the blind stipend. No matter how I reminded him of that, he never went to take care of himself. He had been legally blind since he was four or five years old. Him and my sister Latanya both. They can't see a lick if you take their glasses.

This last time I know a friend of his bought his glasses, because Shane called me when he was ordering him online and I had to give him the password from last time.

This same friend that bought his glasses sent him $100 to my Cash App, and of course I had to ride down to the Northside from Ballwin, Missouri (25 minutes away). I handed him the money through my cracked car window with a mask and gloves, for the prevention of catching the coronavirus. He smiled and said, "I knew you would bring me some gloves and a mask." I told him, "Love you and get yourself together, Shane." I watched him walk back in the apartment and then drove off, back to Ballwin.

It really broke my heart to see him like that. When Shane was five years old, he was smart as a whip to be five years old. I taught him how to remember his timetables up to 5X. He was too smart for himself. He wore those thick eyeglasses too.

Shane is my heart and still is, and that's why I chose tough love, because he knew better. He always has a plan in his head, but that heroin got my baby brother. He almost overdosed twice. Somebody found him unconscious on the back of a truck and called the ambulance. Then I got a phone call from him while he was at the hospital. My heart sank when he told me the story. I thanked God for his life. See, I had been thinking and dreaming about him for a couple of weeks before the overdose. He stayed on my mind.

I was fighting with myself about "Why him, Lord? He is smart and yet must not be wise enough yet to stop with the heroin." I didn't run to his rescue because I had tried to do that over again and I was tired of him calling on me like I was his mother. Yes, I know, I played the role at an early age and at age 51 I'm over tired of the role. Nevertheless, I bought Shane clothes, glasses, and personal items and gave him money for bus fare and extra change in his pocket for interviews.

Lord knows I've prayed over his deliverance from drugs and let these job interviews be positive for him. I was even getting calls on my cell phone, because he had sent out his resumé that I typed up and/or edited when he needed it. My phone was the answering service for all my siblings.

I would call around looking for Shane and any of my siblings. I would have even my mother's calls/messages that came to my phone too. Despite not hearing from my siblings for a while, I was reaching out to them or who was connected to the ones that was on the streets from the last time I knew their whereabouts. My brother and mother knew where to come to be known that they were alive. They gave their new numbers and where and who they were living with and if they were working. This was a continuous thing as of this present day. Two of my younger brothers are presently living in St. Louis and the other in Wentzville, Missouri, with his girlfriend, and the baby brother, with his wife for some years now.

The one that was supposed to be the one they looked up to, besides their dad (no-good). Even my oldest brother (biological) wasn't there, but he wanted to be because he has a heart of gold, selfless and kind, but he was content with the life he was living after getting out of prison after 22 years in 2010. So, we just leave him be, because he doesn't need to be around a lot so he can stay out of trouble. He would go to bat for his siblings, though. Lord knows we couldn't stand for him to go back to prison. We had already lost him for 22 years. He did know a lot about what was going on until he came around and that was when we would tell him the rundown of everybody. Life now from what we knew. He would give us that big handsome smile and hug us so hard when he came around.

Got Through the Pain

> The pain of losing my Grandma Lil at 84 years old on January 10, 2014; and niece, Anijah Renee Shelley-Baldwin (August 11, 2014 – April 17, 2015), the oldest and youngest of the Shelley family, was devastating.

I wish my sister Malenda would seek help with the loss of her baby girl. I have tried to talk to her too many times, to seek therapy. I even told her that I would go with her to therapy. Her two girls and son need the therapy too. But I think they're stronger than their mother, though. The coroner said that baby girl didn't suffer.

I never gave up wanting my sister and her children to seek therapy. But I did give up talking about seeking help for her mental state. It hurt me so much that I could never bear the pain again of going to any of my niece's birthdays or death anniversaries. I believe now she understands why, but before I knew she didn't. But that was alright with my soul, because I had learned through therapy not to take on things that weren't good for my mental state.

15 Years

My sister Latanya had been on crack for 15 years and went back on it in December 2018. I couldn't believe it, and I had cried to my husband. I was so sad. We were back together as sisters, after five years of her out of my life, due to all the drama of our father's death. I tell you, she had stabbed me in my heart with the news. But lo and behold, she came back around out of the crack habit in January 2020. Yes, she had lost everything in her apartment and some while she was on crack. Now she is the Latanya I knew during the 15 years' sober and after the year of going back out there on crack.

Chapter 15

WHO AM I?

You know, I was so confused at an early age and so at an older age, I was still confused about if it was and is my role to care so much about my siblings as hard as I did. Either I care or suffer from not caring. See, I told you I was confused. I didn't know who I was. I was conformed into another person at an early age. What did I know about decision making to a point of caring for my siblings like I was their mother? There, I said it!

I am just starting to figure myself out. I am just finding out who I am, because I had been somebody that my mother molded me. Life had just begun for me when I was getting to know who I was. It was a known joke because I'm back and forth with finding out. I didn't know Janlisa Parris existed. I didn't even know it was a path that would take me to being me. I fought and fought the push to find me. I put my feet still on the beginning of the path and wouldn't break the stillness of my feet to move forward.

It may have been later in my life, 2005, since I really seek help, yet I did. It has been 15 years since I have been seeing a psychiatrist/therapy for mental health. I wasn't ashamed and I made sure my siblings knew. Maybe they would seek mental health care. Only Latanya has to seek care, I know. When I'm around them I make it known what me and my counselor talked about. There was nothing to be ashamed of because I was able to talk and let the wrong feelings out of me that someone else did to me. Yes, I take depression and anxiety medications. Oh, my God, it's been and still is the best to have someone listen and not judge you. To bring out the you in you. To tell you if you're going in the right direction of thinking.

They give you skills to build from and help you grow for the betterment to yourself. With the help of God in the will of helping myself is a blessing. My psychiatrist would increase my medication when need be. I have been on three types of medication in the past 15 years from being diagnosed with depression and anxiety. Well, if you agree or not, you must trust someone that willing to help you. It is been so well for the soul and help in the spiritual realm of thinking. If you know and you need it, I recommend getting some psychiatrist/therapist care. I could cry every time I went see my therapist because if I had known this sooner about what a therapist could help me with my mental state, I would have been a part of it. I was really losing it! No one knew what I was fighting upon myself. I really don't care how anyone thinks and feels about me seeing a therapist. See, this is the new me. Not giving a shit how another person feels or thinks about me.

I hold my head up then and I really hold it up now. Despite my situation in my years of this life, I've always held my head up. This little young 11/12-year-old girl was a powerful young queen with my spiritual strength that was out of this world. Yes, something out of this world is how I see it for me back then. I had never seen myself that way until the therapist. It took me until now, presently, to see the strength and power I have over my own mind.

Going through finding myself and getting to know who I am is not a walk in the park. More like walking on coal and can't reach the end. I tell you, I kept the old ways of my younger years caring about my grown siblings. They knew how to get me because I was all they knew to run to. From what they believed.

I remember, I told myself that I was going to tell my siblings that I'm not God when they called me with their issues and problems. Yes, I did it, but it was very hard when I got off the phone with each of them. They figured after a period went by that they could call me up again. I said, "I'm not God." I can't fix their issues and situation at that time of them reaching out to me by phone.

For 16 years I've had the same cell phone number. It would have been more years, but I had to see how the telecommunication company I worked for a minute. I immediately switched back as soon as I could go back to my last telecommunication company.

I wanted to walk the path that God has ordained for me. I always knew it was more of me, but where is she? Who am I? I fought to find me. Therapy has been a super charge of self-energy, self-peace, self-love, and a lot of self-wisdom.

Wanted to Be Loved Unconditionally Too

Giving my last, caring always, and not caring about self the most. This was what love was to me. I gave all of me and felt I didn't have any love in return. I cared unconditionally, whereas I didn't know to care for myself afterwards. I felt it all was gone.

My spirit said, "Fight, Lisa, Jan, Janlisa, Janlisa Shelley, Janlisa Shelley-Bell, and Janlisa Parris, fight!!! You are in there somewhere. You can't fight this by yourself," my spirit said. "You won't see an end to the madness if you don't start the self-love therapy." Reversing my years of trauma is what I thought, why, I don't know. But what it was, is to say to myself it's not my fault things are the way they are and were. It is okay to just say no to family. It was the hardest thing I ever had to do to my family (siblings). If I'm succeeding in life, I wanted them to succeed too. That is fine, but they must want to succeed for themselves. I wanted so bad for my siblings to have more than I had. See, there I go thinking like a mother. They are not my children, but who would have never known? I am just their sister!

Any time of the day in a 24-hour period, I would answer the phone if my siblings called me on the house or cell phone. I would leave my house with my son to run to their rescue. Not thinking for our overall safety. But safety first, like the military taught me. What I found out I was, I thought while in therapy. No, I was just mimicking the behavior of a mother, with most mothers. I was taught the behavior at an early age, again I say. Something like this is/was very hard to let go. I didn't know I was blocking or enhancing their futures per God's wishes. Again, I didn't know any better than what I was taught. Protecting them was the world to me, while raising my own son. Therefore, therapy was a battle for me, but I must remind myself, they're not my responsibility.

God sent some awesome friends in my life near and far since summer at Soldan 1982, Westside, St. Louis, and since 1987 fall quarter at ASU. Far as I know, these friends have loved me unconditionally. They all have always shown love and concern whenever I was in a negative state of mind and situation. I can call or go by their house in the middle of the night and they will open their doors and let me in and give me a bed to lay my head. They will wait to talk until the morning. These situations are vice versa too. If I call or they call 24/7, there is not a time that the phone will be answered if I am on caller I.D. I know most of these situations in my life will come to a shock but some they know. God saved me!!! I was really a confused case under all that red hair, there was a young girl, then a mother and a wife.

Chapter 16

I AM NOT GOD

March 9, 2020, at 11:16 A.M., as I received a call on my cell phone coming in, I saw that it was my brother (third from the last). I instantly thought, *Damn, why me call somebody else, shit.* But I did answer the phone. He said, "Hey, Lisa, you got Momma number?" UHH! I said, "Hold on while I get it off the phone." Then I told him, "You're pitiful, coming into your baby boy's life, taking him to his games and you disappear." I did tell him not to call me anymore and I'd never give him anything. He is so sad. He makes me sick to my stomach. He has a person that will help him, but he doesn't want the help. I don't want him to get himself together for me. He has a son in elementary school and he really needs his father. I did give him Momma's number, though.

March 9, 2020: My mother was at my sister Malenda's house. I went to take her some Vitamin C packs and cold/flu medicine from over the counter. Because this coronavirus is at pandemic impact. My mom, being 74 years old, just really scares me about her health. She has chronic bronchitis/asthma. While I was there, I did let her know what I told her son over the phone when he called to get her number. You see how I'm looking out for my mother? I can't help it. Honor thy father and mother is one of my values, and I can't honor her no matter what.

Believe me, I am doing this because I'm only human and I know that I did hate my mother only because of how she made me be a caregiver at an early age. Need I say!

It was when in the 15 years of me going to therapy that I was being psyched to understand a lot of things I had gone through, because of a selfish mother. It was time then I wouldn't answer the phone when she called. Then it was time when I was letting her get on my damn nerves badly by answering her phone calls. This caused me to go back to when I was a baby and she left me all shitty and Grandma Lil had to rescue me. It took me back to when I told her I had my menstrual for the first time. I used to talk smart during the phone calls. I didn't care how she felt of being out in the streets sleeping on the park bench or over her friend's elderly home and she needed cigarettes and food. I would tell her, "Momma, you are doing what you want to do, and I can't stop you; you must want to stop for yourself."

Many times I cried while in therapy. There was so much hurting in me due to my mother and her selfish decisions. My mother knew better. She was a mother bully because she knew she had a strongminded daughter that loved her brothers and sister to the moon and back. My mother took that chance every time she could to use me up. Oh, and she used me up, alright, mentally and physically. Physically, because I was stressed where my back would hurt, and my digestion system was all haywire. When I returned to therapy I talked about my mother and dealt with her all throughout my therapy. But most recently, I've not talked about her at all. It has switched to me talking about my brother. I'm going to have to because I just can't turn him off. He was like my child through the years.

My anxiety is real! I can't wait to see my therapist to deal with my siblings on my mind and calling on me. But I must see that they too were messed up from Momma leaving them while she roamed the street. Also leaving them in my care, yet I took on the responsibility because I couldn't see it any other way.

I only had my grandmother, yet I didn't bother her with talking about my situation because she knew my situation already. She was there in the middle of it. Her tears and hurt became my tears and hurt. My Grandma Lil was a mentally strongminded African- American woman, though. My granny lived for 84 years with the stress of her daughter on her mind. My siblings and I couldn't even find our mother when her mother was in critical condition, down in Dothan, Alabama, at Flowers Hospital in ICU.

There have been plenty of nights that I have cried out to the Lord to help me mentally. I knew this was the only way to keep me mentally sane.

I remember, one day I had gotten my student loan refund check and I went to my bank to cash it. Then I came back to get in the car, and as I was sitting in the car God spoke to me and said, "Haven't I been taking care of you? Go back in there and get that cashier's check for your son's tuition!" I jumped out that car and went to get the cashier's check. Yes, God has taken care of me and my son 100% of the way through my life with Dantrell Dior' Shelley. I also remember when I didn't have any money for gas, because I was getting unemployment due to not working for the school system. I was wondering how I was going to barely make it home. I had to pick up Dantrell from little league football practice after I left my bootcamp class at the YMCA. But lo and behold, I had got in the car and started it, and my gas hand went over to three-quarters of a tank of gas. I immediately called my girlfriend in Bronx, New York, to tell her the grace that God had just blessed me with. We both screamed and praised God.

Chapter 17

MIND OVER MATTER

I remember, when my mother said that she was raped while she was out in the streets. I can believe her, because the way she's been and still out in the street for the past 34+ years. She said that she was tied up, raped and let go, by the known St. Louis Rapist that was caught and sentenced to jail, yet he died in prison by suicide. He had targeted sex workers and women of color as his victims (medium.com).

Just knowing your mother is out there selling her body is a mental disaster and that she doesn't care about nothing but crack. She has been arrested so many times for prostitution and let go. It is sad when the police officer knows her name by her face, and full name at that. March 14, 2020, at 4:02 A.M., this woman called me on Saturday morning, asking me to send by Cash App her $10, so she could get the cash off her card and catch the bus home. I sent the money. Then a few minutes later, she called back and asked for $3 because there was a fee at the service station, and so I sent the $3. Then she called back for the third time and said to just send $20 because she was going to use the ATM to get the money. I sent her $15. What a fool I was, because day two after she called me there was no Momma at home. What a liar! She makes me sick to my stomach. I know it was my fault because I should have known better not to send her any type of money amount. Really,

I thought she was crying to get home, especially at 4:02 A.M. because recently and for months she had been coming home after one or two days being out. She had been out for one day this time.

I stopped by my sister Malenda's house that morning of Momma's call and Momma wasn't there still. But she had the nerve to call my phone and ask if she had gotten any mail. Yes, she wanted to know if her Personal Tax Credit (PTC) refund check had come in through the mail. I said no and hung up the phone. I am so pissed at myself for sending the money to her and I should know damn better. The enemy tried to find something to attack me, but that was small, yet big. I bet it's the last time I do that again.

Sunday evening, she called again while I was at my sister's house again, after church. She started to explain that she was at her friend's (male) house with him. She said, "He called me before I got on the bus and I went to see him." I said, "I don't care, and you need to stop lying and you need to get a life." Then I hung up the phone on her. I really didn't care if her feelings were hurt or not. She is a disgrace to herself, children, and society.

Grandma Lil is not here to see what she's still doing.

My sister had her grandchildren over to her house and I didn't want Momma to come to her house because we didn't know if she was around someone with the coronavirus. No telling who she was around. Sleeping with and touching that's sick. What do she care, because as you see she out in the streets. I was glad that my niece came to get her children before Momma showed up, when she did show up. My baby sister, Malenda, got some choice words for her when she does come home, off those streets. Me too. Because I'm going to give her a piece of my mind.

Believe me, I'm going to keep my distance. I surely don't trust her surroundings and whereabouts on the Northside of St. Louis. I don't know how she is getting her crack. She still doesn't care and always thought about herself. I can't do her as a friend, and you may be thinking the opposite because she's my mother. Like I said and I'll say it again, she is a disgrace to be a mother of seven children!

You are saying, does this woman have anything good about her? Well, yes, she does. When crack is not her mission now, I guess because I don't know for sure. Annie Jean Shelley is giving and has a good heart! Done! I can't say too much about her goodness because I'm still confused about who she really is as a sober human being. Yet, she puts on, so I can forget all of what she put me through throughout my life. I do forgive her, but it so hard because I'm always forgiving her within myself.

I must listen to her say I'm sorry, why, just another thing to make me sick to my stomach, again.

My mother has not completely lost herself in the crack. I say this because she was brought up in the foundation of knowing better, back home in Enterprise, Alabama, by her grandparents on both sides of her mother and father. She told me that she used to sleep on the church bench because she went there through the week and on Sundays. Her grandfather (Rev. Brady Whitehurst, August 17, 1903 – January 7, 1980) was a sanctified preacher. If her grandparents could see her now, they would be so disappointed, like I am.

March 16, 2020: Annie Jean Shelley (Momma) came home after three days in the streets walking around. My sister Malenda saw her Sunday night at 1:30 P.M. at the service station. Malenda said, "She tried to hide her face by playing in her hair," and that she knew her walk. Malenda confronted her by telling her, "You better have your stamps," and my momma said, "I have them and you aren't getting my card." Then Malenda said, "You going to need some food when you get home, so you better have them."

High as a Kite

I arrived over my sister Malenda's house that afternoon and I started to go downstairs in her little room area and wake her up, but I didn't. I decided I didn't want the drama because I was going to chew her out about my money. Well, that money went on crack. I wanted to tell her off about her having the coronavirus while she been walking the street and doing who know what to get her crack. She is a sick individual.

Do you all know, she had the darn nerves to lie and say she was going and meet her daughter-in-law at the bus stop to give her some money. The next thing you know, she was calling asking me if she got any mail, then I asked her if she had gotten tested for the coronavirus. Oh, she hung up on me. Malenda told her when she called her to not come back to her house until she got tested. Momma had the nerve to call and tell Latanya that she paid her way to live there and she didn't know why she couldn't come back to the house. My sister told her that she was not in it; therefore, she had nothing to say about the situation. Then the next day, my mother called me and asked if I could call the IRS to see if her PTC check was processed. I said, "No, I'm not calling nobody," and I hung up on her, and she told me that she was at her daughter-in-law's house. She told me that she had been trying to contact Malenda. Yet, she finally reached her and the next day she was back at my sister's house. I was praying that she wouldn't bring the coronavirus in my sister's house.

I can't end to tell you all that I have left some things out, but only for conversation piece! To give you everything means there's nothing to talk about if I'm interviewed.

My sisters, Latanya and Malenda, are doing great these days. My brothers are alive and I haven't seen the last two baby brothers in a while. I haven't seen my oldest brother but my sister Latanya has seen him. Yes, all my mother's children are alive these days. That is why I don't understand how she can't stop what she's doing in the streets. She has made it to age 73 and has 26 grands/greats altogether. I can say that about her children too. We have always been afraid that our momma would die from crack overdose on the streets. I really used to be intense in my younger years. Yes, we don't know how she will leave us now, but if it is by overdose, then we're not afraid anymore. God has given us the 70s, yet we do want more. I want to give her a 75th birthday celebration, just like I gave her a 70th celebration in 2016 at my home and it was a successful evening of love.

Our Home

Even in 2018/'19 she came to live with me and had everything from her own bedroom/TV/and she could cook whatever she wanted. Pretty much our home was her home. She came to me and told me, "I'm finished with that stuff, and can I come live with you and Darrel?" I had gotten all her appointments scheduled to go to her doctor's. She was scheduled to see a dentist and get her new teeth. I took her shopping for new clothes all the time; either it was at a department store or secondhand store, she had plenty of clothes and items she needed, and some wants too. I was excited for her. She meditated out in the fully closed sunroom that she could see the backyard and other yards too. My husband made her feel so comfortable and that we were happy to have her in our home. He always brought her favorite snacks and foods when he went to the store. There was nothing she couldn't do in our home that would make us want to see her go, except doing crack again. Far as she knew we enjoyed Momma being in our home.

Unfortunately, she turned on herself and went back to the streets, but she knew that there would always be a bed if she became drug free. Our home was still her living address that was used on all her mail. There she was back cracking! SMDH!!!

My Veil

Was ripped and torn on May 22, 1993, before 12 P.M. when I delivered my son, Dantrell (26 hours later, 7 pounds, 4 ounces, shoulders and neck wide and head was 13 cm (huge); and I was split from the rudder to the tudder with 22 stitches). The pain was severe as my mother sat on the side of the bed holding my hand. My girlfriend came to visit me before going to our other girlfriend's wedding. I had suffered from Bell's palsy overnight while in the hospital. I knew whatever journey I was getting ready to walk through wasn't going to be alone. I was a fighter and had the mental strength of determination within me. It was just overwhelming juggling my own life, son's, and siblings' so they could have a decent life outside of the one they had lived thus far.

My momma had the nerve to tell me that now that I think about the time, that (no-good) man beat my son in his bedroom, that she hated that she let that happen. I told her that she should be hurting about it. I didn't have any remorse of what I said, either. Then I told her, "Please be quiet, Momma." See, I needed peace now because it brought up unhealthy not mindfulness moments in my life. Sometimes I can't stand to be around my mother, as you already know. Memories still come up, but they don't rule my day or moment when I think about my past. I can't tell you of the horrible things she did and let happen to her children, when we looked to her to protect and be gentle to us when we deserved it and rightfully so.

61